D0292404

The Lions
and the Water Buffaloes

Story by Beverley Randell *Illustrations by Julian Bruère*

Five little lion cubs
played together every day.
Their mothers took care of them
all the time.
They were too small
to take care of themselves.

The mother lions
always hid their cubs
under the bushes,
or under the trees,
or in the long grass
to keep them safe.

One hot day,
the mother lions
hid their cubs under some trees.
The cubs went to sleep.

Then all the big lions
went to sleep out in the sun.

Soon a herd of water buffaloes
came along.
They saw the lion cubs
lying in the grass.

The herd tried to go around them.

One of the mother lions woke up.
The water buffaloes
were too close to the cubs!
She had to save them.

The mother lion
raced over to the water buffaloes
and tried to scare them away.

But the water buffaloes
were not scared of just one lion.

The water buffaloes had great horns
that could toss her
out of the way.

The mother lion could not save
the cubs by herself.

Another mother lion
came to help her.
But the water buffaloes
just kept on coming.

If the water buffaloes
came any closer,
they might step on the cubs
and kill them.

Then the father lion
opened his mouth and **roared**!
He ran at the water buffaloes.
He looked much bigger
than the mother lions.

The water buffaloes were not scared
of one or two lions,
but now **three** lions
were trying to chase them away.

They turned and ran off.

The mother lions
ran under the trees,
and called to their five cubs.

But only three little cubs
came running out.

Two of them were missing!
The mother lions ran up and down
looking for their cubs.

At last the mother lions
could hear the cubs crying.

The cubs were too scared
to come out of the long grass
where they had run to hide.

But they had not been hurt at all.
The three lions had saved the cubs,
just in time.